THIS UNICORN BOOK BEL

....

How Did I Catch A Unicorn?
My Unicorn Books - Volume 1
Written by Steve Herman

Copyright © 2019 by Digital Golden Solutions LLC.
Published by DG Books Publishing, an imprint of
Digital Golden Solutions LLC.

Information contained within this book is for entertainment and educational purposes only. Although the author and publisher have made every effort to ensure that the information in this book was correct at press time, the author and publisher do not assume and hereby disclaim any liability to any party for any loss, damage, or disruption caused by errors or omissions, whether such errors or omissions result from negligence, accident, or any other cause.

ISBN: 978-1-950280-06-3 (paperback)
ISBN: 978-1-950280-07-0 (hardcover)

www.MyUnicornBooks.com

First Edition: July 2019
10 9 8 7 6 5 4 3 2 1

HOW DID I CATCH A UNICORN?
MY UNICORN BOOKS - VOLUME 1
STEVE HERMAN

I'm Allyson McNally, but since that's a lot to say,
Folks just call me Allie, which is better anyway.
I can tell you something that you won't believe, I'll bet –
Okay, here goes – I have a unicorn for a pet!

A unicorn is not the sort of pet that you can buy;
You can't adopt them at the pound, and I can tell you why –

Picking out a unicorn is something one can't do –
No, you must wait with patience for one to come to you.

But don't expect a unicorn to walk right in your door,
For waiting's not enough – No, it takes something more.
I can see that you are wondering, "Allie, how'd you do it?"
Well, once you know the secret, there's really nothing to it!

ABOUT A YEAR AGO...

Listen closely and I'll tell you how it came to be
That a real live unicorn came to live with me.

It was about a year ago, my attitude was bad;
I wanted to be happy, but was always getting mad.

One day I got angry with my little brother, Ben;
He broke my favorite mermaid doll, I yelled at him and then

Mom put me in time-out, which made me madder than before –
I cried and stomped my foot, and then I slammed
my bedroom door!

When we were at the store, I saw a doll I wished I had,
But dad wouldn't buy it, 'cause I'd been acting bad.

I asked again, and he said, "No!" - I threw another fit,
Then I cried myself to sleep, but it didn't help a bit.

At school I loaned my favorite pencil to my classmate, Tim,
But Tim was careless and he lost it – I was so mad at him!

"You better find my pencil,
or say you're SORRY, Tim!" I said,
But Tim thought that was funny
and stuck out his tongue, instead!

After that, for days and days, I wore an angry frown.
My parents asked, "Allie, don't you think
it's time that you calm down?"

The next week was no better; things went from bad to worse.
I was the most unhappy child in all the universe!
"A magic unicorn," I said "I think might be the key
To take away my anger and bring happiness to me."

The other children laughed and said, "Allie, don't you know
That unicorns are fairy tales!" - I knew better, though!
I believe in unicorns! It seems I always knew
There is magic in the world. Do you believe it, too?

I KNEW BETTER THOUGH!

THERE'S MAGIC IN THE WORLD.

But no one else believed;
that made me madder still.
I continued feeling angry
that whole day until...
Later from my window,
I was looking out that night –
I saw a flock of unicorns –
such a wondrous sight!

A sparkling flock of unicorns
beneath my apple tree -
The stars were twinkling in their eyes
as they looked back at me.
Oh, how I wished to touch one,
but much to my dismay,
The unicorns took fright and then they swiftly flew away.

At my window every day, I would watch and wait to see
If the flock of unicorns might come back to visit me.

A unicorn came sliding down, and much to my surprise,
There stood a lovely unicorn, right before my eyes!

I tip-toed oh so softly, then stepped out my back door –
But she did not run away like the unicorns before.

I said, "My name is Allie. Would you take me for a ride?!"
But when I stepped up to pet her, she gently stepped aside.

I asked, "If I can't touch you, then why did you return?"
She said, "Because you need me. There's something you must learn."

Then I told her of my brother, Ben,
and things that he had done;
And how I got in trouble, and I wasn't having fun.

I told her of the kids at school and Ms. Johnson, too –
"No wonder, I am mad," I said, "What's a girl to do?!"

"Please help me with your magic. I'm so tired of being mad,"
But Dazzle D. replied, "Allie, you have always had..."

"The magic in yourself to make the anger go away –
I'll tell you how to do it, then you can start today."

"For instance, when you find yourself getting mad at Ben,
Before you start to yell at him, stop and count to ten."

"And when you want a toy, ask your dad how you can earn it
That's better than a tantrum, and it's time for you to learn it."

"Don't get caught up in the drama
with the other kids at school;
Remember why you're there;
that will help you keep your cool."

"Some things make us angry,
but there's something you should know -
You can't let your anger linger;
you must let your anger go."

"Be careful when you're angry of the things you do and say.
Remember it will pass, and don't let it ruin your day."

"Life is meant to be enjoyed;
don't spend it being mad.
When you are calm, then I'll return.
Allie, you'll be glad!"

But I remembered all the things that Dazzle D had said,
And put a smile upon my face and read a book, instead.

So I practiced Dazzle D's advice and saw that she was right. Guess who came to see me on another moonlit night!

I ran to my back yard where I saw Dazzle D,
With a smile upon her face and waiting there for me.

When she saw how calm I had become,
Dazzle D was proud.
"Do you still want a ride?" she asked.
"Now you are allowed!"

That's how I caught a unicorn,
and now she's my best friend.
If you'd like to catch one, too,
then I strongly recommend...
That you choose to take control
over what you say and do.
Only calm girls and boys can catch a unicorn -
If I can, so can you!

Get your FREE Gift from Dazzle at
www.MyUnicornBooks.com/gift

READ MORE ABOUT ALLIE AND DAZZLE!

My Unicorn Books - Volume 1

My Unicorn Books - Volume 2

VISIT
WWW.MYUNICORNBOOKS.COM

Made in the USA
Coppell, TX
06 December 2019